Today I Found the River

jazz poems by elizabeth gordon mckim

LILY POETRY REVIEW BOOKS

Published by Lily Poetry Review Books
223 Winter Street
Whitman, MA 02382

https://lilypoetryreview.blog/

ISBN: 978-1-957755-67-0

Table of contents

At first whole continents

Archipelago. Savanna. Promontory. Great Plains. Delta.
Death Valley. Northeast kingdom. Mississippi. Badlands.
Devil's Gulch.
The great Missouri.
Juan de Fuca. The Straits.
Swallow. Swallowing song
A way. Far off.
Birds early in the easy rising.
Owl. Raven. Cormorant.
The swallow.
sw sw
wallowing near
The hippo mud-slashing
Sloshing shing shing
tear crystal flake leaf speck dot
sw sw
winging
all
owing/allowing
no thing *st st*
uck uck
only
you
this singular
song you are
singing
in the muck of it

uprising

Motion/Commotion

For Etheridge Knight

I like to mosey
You like to mill

You like to rumble
I like to spill

I like to gallivant
you like to gamble

I like to sally forth
you like to ramble

I like to hushaby
you like to drum

you like to signify
I like to hum

I like to gadabout
You like to layabout

I like to glide about
You like to slide about

I like to hushaby
You like to steam

You like to roustabout
I like to dream

Awash

with these moonshines
                Fully in the great
sexual mind of things
                As you said
        We are all a part
Of that one great nation
                It holds us
And we whisper to it
        Like sea creatures
We lurch into the tide
        into the clear amazement
where the poem has trailed off
        burned through
                Is it our fault
                        We prefer to dance?

For Ferrini

Poetry Class

you have to imagine
the cage you have to imagine
the room the children piling into it the fighting
you have to imagine the room and the door closing
and they coming in yelling and fighting
their high voices filling the space
and i am sitting in the middle playing a kalimba
saying *peace* and they look at me as if I speak a language
they cannot understand they converge like hungry
starlings on the colored stones I bring for them
to touch

you have to imagine
them swinging their fists
piling on top of each other you have to
imagine them crowding me and I knowing there is no more
room for them to move
and the sound of the kalimba and they say
please miss tell us how to spell
shit tell us how to spell
burn and the teacher
says *ok you guys*
if you don't want to be quiet
he is shouting now and the colored stones
are breaking I hear myself saying
don't touch the stones they'll break and a voice
from behind says *why'd you bring 'em*
if you don't want us to break 'em and one of the kids
dances over to the closet yanks out a red cloth
and a cymbal he throws his head back
he's chanting in his red cape
clanging and he's high

and sally whose brother hung himself
two weeks ago is wrapped around a poem
about a bird trying to get free
and I am sitting here
playing nothing
now

Brockton MA, 1972

Angel

Well I really didn't want to approach this one
the huge one the high honcho
the big guy the cell boss of angels the one
I have been leaning/toward/leading/up to/the one
in the corner/the one who swoops/and flails/and flips
the one who veers/the one who means business
the workaholic one the one
who never goes to miami the one you knew was in the room
the one I knew was in the room the one who did not leave
the one you tried to smote the one i tried to smote
the one who finally wrapped its wings around you
as you breathed your way into me convulsing
as you flew light and easy as you swarmed
out the window singing *ride ride*
no i am going to leave this
alone i am going
to stop here

singing

Bee Holding

1

Where's the honey bee
Now the colony's collapsed?
Is clover/over?

2

Saw a bee fly by my head
   it was burning
Heard my own small girl
   swallowing the sunlight
she was humming
   Lately I've been turning
to the ringing
   through the window
Today outside the springtime
   well I almost tasted snow
We were frozen splinters once
There's a bee above my head
   It's calling riding
Had a lover once
   and never told my husband
Saw his face above my bed
Heard a bell inside my head

   Lately/I've been/dying
   for the/honey/in the stinging
   Lately/I've been/dying
   for the/honey/in the stinging

3

I held it in my hand.
It didn't sting or fly away.

In fact it stayed
through all that season
till the weather swarmed and changed.
I didn't know what it could mean
or why I cried.

4

Outside our door a brogue of bees astir in the honey
till dark when the wind shoves through unhinges the cage
turns pale deposits me out of bounds where animals run
their eyes alive with fright. I come to find the fire.
I follow the humming to the bush. Nothing is left.
I run to the witching stones the land bleeds dry
I reach for the sky
the sky scoops me up
spits me back I splinter in blades
of grass I lie through my teeth
when I tell
honey
bees I like
to lie in the sun
moving bees alive in the sun
a bush in the sun in the heat alive with bees

There are bees in sarajevo there are bees in prague
there are bees in chicago and soweto there are
bees in santiago there are bees in belfast
there are bees in boston even as we speak
there are bees there are bees
bees on their way to you yes to you
It's not a secret anymore

About Dreaming
Note to my students

I too

      have dreamed up a storm

           toppled my father

                beat someone I loved

          into a bloody pulp

       turned my momma into ash

changed into a one-eyed hawk

       disappeared into morning

           melted the mirror

I too

      arrived at school without my clothes

          and I have run

                 and remained

         in the same old dirt

Bee Loved

I held it in my hand
It didn't sting or fly away
In fact it stayed
until the weather swarmed
and changed
I didn't know
what it could mean
or why I cried

hilaya
highlea
ling ling
long may
the long
flat days
bee

        i have clock-
        grouch he said
        complainin'
        leanin' toward her

        funny she said
        i have dreamt
        lusciously…triumphantly
        of humpbacked proceedin's
        honey and oranges

            hilaya
                highlea

I have tracked you far over the meaning-
less white snows I have pursued you into
other people's barns I have stopped at night
to hear the chill strangeness of your call

> eventually you shall eat me too
> and our bones shall flower and rise

> and we shall walk in the morning
> into the sudden plausibility
> of our city

Change In The Air

The creatures
Are trying out
Their new-
Found
Gestures
Every
Which way
Like penguins.

Nothing
Perfunctory.
Only these
Succinct
Hard-won
Motions.
The architects of new meanings
Excite the frozen air
Exit with unsuspected eloquence
Flapping their possibilities
Like prayer flags

Like prayer flags

Where I am
You are
In this fabulous tableau

Look ahead now…
The creatures are taking
Their bows

Brag Swag

I got my P.H.D.
In O.L.D.
And I'm tough
I'm tender
I'm a poetry defender
I'm weak I'm wild
an ancient child
I'm a big time winner
an epic failure
I'm la creme de la creme
I'm a desperado
In an eldorado
I'm an old crusader
a cradle raider
I'm a cougar
With no luger
I'm a walker I'm a talker
I'm a big time squawker
I'm a lover
Under cover
I'm adorable deplorable
Dependable and durable
A ready made renegade
A queen of spades
A jacky of the trades
I got my P.H.D.
In O.L.D.

And I'm yours!

Cops In The Kitchen

There were cops
In the kitchen that day
Bigger than bassoons or tubas
They carried my cousin away
They said they had received complaints
She chanted: and worse:
In a weird wired language
They could not comprehend
The men tramped around the premises
Switching on the lights
Terrifying dust and mice
Before they found her in the kitchen
Chanting up a storm:
Ways to baffle men
Or stall the tide
Or make a stew
And when the cops came in
The mice scampered sideways
The dust billowed
The stew onion-swarmed
Spilled upon the floor
And burned the skidding soles
Of the cursing men
The cops blew whistles
My cousin laughed
And split her sides
The tears ran out
To inundate the kitchen
Of the infidels

Letter

For Don White

I want to send
You a letter
You have never received
I want to send it
In the morning
At first light
But if I have to
I will send it at noon
Or I will send it
if need be
At dusk
or even if I must
I will send it at midnight
Or in the lost hours of the wolf
When you can not sleep

I want to know the sound of your steps
In the city where you survive
I want to know how you breathe
in the space between
the moments

one leaf
its jagged edge
one stone
scarred

One face
at the broken
window

I want to know your evenings
and how they spread out before you
And your mornings the sound of your starlings
I want to know your ragged stars

Haikus for Late December

Day and night the bright
Sound of bells in the cradle
between two mountains

Waxes and wanes
In the exact middle of things
where the riddle remains

Tin/tin/abulation
in the valley between joy
and desolation woe and

jubilation

Invitation

Come in around *the friendly fire,* my love, breathe free;
and hold these poems a while, for you
and yes, for me.

It's winter here,
we seek a warming trend,
Look, we've moved past the end
and last year's war,
but even now the wind has rubbed
us sore; the babies cry, the wild dogs
bark, scud missiles tearing up the dark.

Begin this poem, my love,
for you, and yes, for me,
It will not save us, or drag us
from the dark, but we can use it
as the children did the crumbs
to cut a path to lead us
where we can not see.

Come in around
the friendly fire, my love,
breathe free. And hold this poem
a while for you, and yes for me.

Watch

In the cusp of loving
I skim lonely
in precise places
near your home I watch you from
up-
side the head from
water-
bed, from book of the dead
from gibbous to full
moon from cow jump
over the salty spoon,
from telephone call from
Duluth, from empty booth, from
forget me, from knot,
from two roads on the earth
both taken from two tongues
shaken/from down/side/under
from easter from birth
from the mirror from
bring home the beacon from
thunder from what we share
from when you look at me
from when I look at you
from mirth from care from when we go home
we go home together two together
gather ro/ses ro/ses

washed in the blood of the lamb
washed in the blood of the lamb

Song

the root is part of the flower
the flower is part of the root

the moon belongs to the water
the water belongs to the moon

the dark earth belongs to the sunlight
the sunlight belongs to the ground

the sound belongs to the silence
the silence belongs to the sound

Today I found the river

I mean it's not as if
It wasn't there before
But I never really saw
How wide it was
And how the water moved it
Not just a short way
Not just a broken way
I mean clear across and over
And the water was light
And suddenly I knew
That I had been preparing for years
First when it was a neat rectangle
Between my eyes
Then when it washed all over me
Like a flood
And now when it's a river I join
It's come from somewhere
It's going somewhere
It's wide
I join it
Now

Acknowledgments

Thank you to the following journals and presses, where these poems first appeared:

Swallowing Song, Kinchafoonee Creek Press, Athens, GA - "At First
    Whole Continents"
Lovers in the Free Fall, Leapfrog Press, 2020 - "Motion/Commotion,"
    "Change in the Air," "Cops in the Kitchen," "Letter," "Watch"
The Red Thread, Leapfrog Press, 2003 - "Angel," "Bee Holding,"
    "Bee Loved"
Family Salt, Wampeter Press, 1981 - "Poetry Class," "About Dream-
ing,"
    "Today I Found the River"
Elizibetheridge - "Invitation," "Song"

About the Author